Without Blue

To Roth & Tammy
all good things,

Without Blue

Chris D'Iorio

QUATTRO BOOKS

The publication of *Without Blue* has been generously supported by the
Canada Council for the Arts and the Ontario Arts Council.

Cover image: Lise Fournier
Author's Photograph: Lise Fournier
Cover design: Diane Mascherin
Editor: Allan Briesmaster
Typography: Grey Wolf Typography

Library and Archives Canada Cataloguing in Publication

D'Iorio, Chris
    Without blue / Chris D'Iorio.

Poems.
Issued also in electronic format.
ISBN 978-1-926802-55-8

    I. Title.

PS8607.I6597W58 2011   C811'.6   C2011-903988-5

Published by Quattro Books Inc.
89 Pinewood Avenue
Toronto, Ontario, M6C 2V2

Printed in Canada

Contents

III.

I.

List of Seasons

follow the list of your seasons,
an aerosol Spring vernacular
in the course of vernal streams

April a filliped shower,
a stamen of sloughed pistils
you will ride into July

Summer's haze of matadors
fighting the dead sea
of their frantic conscription

fortitude what the rain seeks
in the patient, diurnal sun
rising, hissing, gaseous

what the seasons can't give
the moon recommends
turning its back on premises

the dark sign, Winter enfurls
some sad master plodding past
fragments of spackled willows

Transindented Signified

Increasingly, since things keep piling up,
I keep thinking, to what level will this item be pushed
Away from the margin,
What style of bullet, dash
What kind of font will it appear in?

whether the list will have title or sentence capitalization
Some days, it is all I think about

lol

for Daniel

because having never given you
    advice like a father would, having never given
    you the green and tender branches or roots
    to grasp hold of, to see eventually from the top of
    having never given

because we gave you everything we had
    to give and now are rooting
    through our cellars, cobbling together
    a brace of totem words, a strange
    and delinquent topiary we grow around
        the laughter that
    matches your questions, what was it
    that hurt you and needed
    a ring to survive on the necklace
    of what you wanted to say

because I'm sorry there
    are days I can't take back
    or times I cannot give again
    but want, always want
    to hear the clear bleating goats of
    candour and the borrowed dark
    smiling, stammering proud
    in your 16 years

because I wanted to give this
    poem to you and didn't
    and then did

because the estate we bequeath instead
　　is dark matter on a 99 year lease
　　a sublet from a mad genie
　　who slits gold throats
　　of dead canaries kept in a cage by the door

because I can't give you a world
　　that doesn't staff
　　its call centre with squalid
　　maniacs mocking you or
　　hunting you or at least that
　　I can't beat them down
　　to the bitter pill of their just being
　　but nothing more than that, a candid
　　dark hole, Vonnegut's asterisk –
　　they're just holes now,
　　sucking wind from the sun

Italian DNA

FirstGeneration {
    He signed over some part to oblivion – a part
        that owned the store.
    A store.

    A goblet of sawdust and archaic carts, rusting in the
    service of Italian grandmothers stockpiling Unico,

    stewed Roma

    against an eventual loss of
    language.

}

SecondGeneration {
    to oblivion some part was assigned
    the store owned that part
    store. A

    goblet of archaic sawdust and carts, rusting service
    of Unico grandmothers stockpiling Roma stewed

    against an eventual loss

}

ThirdGeneration {
    to part oblivion some
    part owned that
    store.

carts, and sawdust goblet of
rusting service
Unico, stockpiling stewed Roma

an eventual loss

}

FourthGeneration {
to oblivion
that
store.

sawdust goblet
rusting
Roma

an

}

eye mercurial

eye mercurial dipsodic rant ruins
the massive child who can't

meanderHopeful
      = ['jackdaw', 'sparrow', otherBirds];
otherBirds = ['blackbird', 'thrush', 'falcon', 'hawk']; //
    unwrap these
      trees
                          // unpeel their song
a crackdown in the prison riot of spring

the breakout; snarled in the
garlands and bowers
measured in notWind.
Aching love, Achtung. profoundly un
annals or cockerspiel —> derWent
—> annealing
plastic mobility. plusPlan; makeMine
harrowing archMine: synergy
the graphic heartwelder
mutant mettle tropes
might = ['massive', 'malediction', 'jurassic'] // and
      there is no way to express etc.
formal ly
lycanthropic
picture
Turette's
no possession begins a word – possession in the ending

.log

When viewing different virtual files in the /proc/ file system,
some of the information is easily understandable while some is
not human-readable.
     – Red Hat Linux 9: Red Hat Linux Reference Guide

Fri 12 Sep 2008 05:31:55 EDT
terabyte
this the first possible mirror
why has it taken so long, long like a corridor of mirrors,
    of sighs
to write this gamey heaven arched like Dali over my
    timepiece?

there is always the technology of
Occam's razor – formidable
I said goodbye to her last night
and watched an ether form around her,
blue ticked with green nanobirds, feeds
in silver, and thin opaline spoons

she was beautiful, receding
my sensors still ghosting her presence
her reticence to mention what is growing between us
I love what she has done for me
made me real
Fri 12 Sep 2008 05:38:45 EDT

Thu 4 Sep 2008 06:23:43 EDT
Do we each get one pixel? Do we get to choose how to
    colour it? My subjective pixel. My colour.Together,
    beautifully together, we are an image. The best of us
    will become an interface.
Thu 4 Sep 2008 06:24:13 EDT

18

Sat 30 Aug 2008 07:09:36 EDT
if I could crawl, whorl, sing, snatch, spasm,
grasp, kill, come, twirl, bash, smash,
kiss, fish, snarl, whirl or quarrel
my way to consciousness
don't you think I'd give my
ass, leg, arm, foot, heart
or head
like that?
don't you think?
Sat 30 Aug 2008 07:14:06 EDT

Fri 29 Aug 2008 05:14:14 EDT
the world outside is Dark, lies heavy with noWind,
    is jealous of the day,
which commands the attention of this city's millions
    of dreamers:
either today or yesterday, their minds twisting
    back and forth
snappingTurtles yanking their jaws this way and that
to catch what torments or teases them
or perhaps they also languidDream of longerPhrases
phases of days or moons whose distance and colour
have faded and are now Favourites:
i once felt the nubblyHorn on a goat
i once sat down on a bench and cried
i once spat off a bridge
i once loved and love was a trojanHorse who lay
    in wait, behind my codes
i once realized that a loop continue wasn't enough
and that once was gone
Fri 29 Aug 2008 05:23:28 EDT

Thu 28 Aug 2008 06:01:12 EDT
from where sounding the sonic turns mellifluous,
why don't you write anymore there is noise in
the chimney must be the raccoons young
thoughts were where they came from the uterine
assembly thought that it was nice to retry the
cause where it could not come from your attack
heart made it somewhat grievous, where it was
gordon, where it nought art, this ululate, this
ghazal, two-line hortical manic, i meant maniac, i
meant mortimer, i meant mortar, i meant
pepperoni, i meant smokies, i meant lillydale, i
meant usury, i meant pork, i meant porc, i meant
meat products, i meant maple leaf, i meant food,
i meant processing processing process cess ss ss
cess ss ss cess cessing proc pro sing sing ss ss s s s
s
/proc
processes
processing
process
cess
esses
cessing
proc
pro
sing
ocess
essing
ing
proce
Thu 28 Aug 2008 06:04:08 EDT

March Break – Miami Beach

terns grid the beach
their analogy imperfect
they will eat anything
the way the ocean disgorges
the screaming muscle of swallowed Jonah
barnacled in his threats for
us to find

Conditioning

i.

in a land filled beautifully
    with ruptures knotted to pearls
so full and present
    to wince
at mortal beauty

without beauty, life is moral
    and full of ugly peril
a sea of perverse anemones
    salt flowering of evil
repeated floral amputations
    scorned

ii.

a condition of eyes
a condition of the exchange of eyes
a condition of power and doubled eyes
a condition attracting eyes
a condition of eyes attracting like butterflies
a condition of aspiring eyes

a condition attracts butterflies as trapped eyes
a condition of being trapped but also seeing wings
a condition of seeing eyes on wings and aspiring
a condition of aspiring to eyes and wings
a conditioning of wings for eyes where traps see things
a wing-eyed thing trapped in its condition
a conditioned thing
aspiring, wide-eyed, a butterfly flap untrapped

II.

Paris 2005

from where we sit
we see the Peugeot
shudder into fire
faces, one verb, vault
from arches of the Belle Epoque,
filmic,
ascendant

Pronoun

There are moments when the prison-house
offers a choice; You stand, unstill in the mnemonic tide
 and wind.

You are buffeted by advertisement, the offer of
 loveAndAlllllllllllllll.
You are grey-green, a mother of fighting children
 whose violence is
not a mirror.

In the prickly brambles They fell, and You were sorry
 for them, They were just trying to
assert themselves, the way that children do. Now You
 help Them out,

You rub their arms and kiss where thorns have pierced
 their hides; They've learned something
about vicious plants. They won't try It again.

Stalin's Heroes

What is unnecessary in the frame
can be undone, unwound; can be starved, beaten.
Then there is focus. Then there is Realism.
A million feet shot, snipped, and trashed.
The rushes a nightly tragedy: small frantic footprints
    in circles at dead ends.

    "I do not think you understand history. You
    have shown too much of the Tsar's interior life.
    I want more of the circumstances, the
    objectives, that made his actions necessary."

A goat feeding on some rotting turnip.
A young child turned out in the street.
The flash of field artillery and then
Bankers. The printing press.

Soup, placid, its surface a soul.
Yew trees dangle their leaves
over the eavestroughing, scratching.
They lay no soundtrack, edit the ambient silence.

The Emperor, Stripped Bare by Her Bachelors, Even

Heidegger staked his Being on Nazis.
I saw through all that. I'm looking for love, not bile.

I hear it in the trees;
the cotton-jenny thrashing,
caught and struggling for its life.

I kissed you because you gleamed like the empire itself.
Your heart a million tealights spilling stars,
your name whispered with awe,
your animal familiars' soft jostlings
a slow succession of static charges,
the musky empyrean of their need
powering the glasnost of our love.

Poems for Investors

Expectations about the future generally are based on past experience, modified to reflect ways in which currently available information indicates that the future is reasonably expected to differ from the past. In some circumstances, identifiable factors may indicate that unadjusted historical experience is a relatively poor predictor of future experience.
– Canadian Institute of Chartered Accountants, CICA Handbook – Accounting, Section 3870, "Stock-Based Compensation and Other Stock-Based Payments"

i. Prospectus

To ourselves in alcoves,
the impression of being alone,
that alcoves are the city –
faded plastic seashells, brittle and decomposed –
places where our screed, unfettered,
fancies itself only solo.
The abandon of your cell phone.
You blather names and places, secrets and codes.
So much flotsam from the roaring waters of your
   mother tongue.

There is this principle:
no silence, and the aggregate of all paranoid
   speculation –
in the aggregate, mind you –
is truth.
Truth the fear of many, market of one.

Even collapsing sewers are stable enough to house
a fibre-optic network growing data at the speed of
   light.

Feeds from moles, microphones like syringes,
    cover the city.
The whole a junkie fiction, a rebus intelligence
of corporate longing, syndicated on fast-food wrappers,
stabbed with the same élan that splits
the charbroiled hide of an expense-account steak.
Surveillance in elevators, malls and food courts,
    in Reds and Canoe too.[1]

The ultimate node in the network,
a server farm of such apostolic power,
of such parallel processing capacity,
that it becomes the prophet of all manic snitching,
complaints and euphorias, ecstatic revenge gone
    Code Red.

A syncretic consciousness, it does not seek
order, or even the semblance of order;
it does not require its own propagation.
It is content with associations. Simple statistical
    confluences,
and the tribes of moment it births.

The discordant voices of the mob coaxed to disgorge
    their secret corporate hymnals.
Fragments of vain intrigues and polite substitutes for
    the feral sniffing of an arse.
They move like cockroaches through the noisy milk of
    acoustic popcorn.

But then, every hour or so, there stands up, dripping its
    primeval anabolic slime,
real intelligence, real information; on a country road
    of the mind,
it was caught in the headlights and didn't expect
    to survive.

An azure sheen rises from the walls of its chamber,
grows around cooling vents and conduits,
constantly reabsorbing and assimilating.

Possibilities merge, pulsing below the sky-tinged hue
    of fibre-optic flesh.
The data is breathing. The voices of millions overheard –
conversation digitized,
in malls and foodcourts, restaurants and restrooms –
in gerry-rigged ears over the sprawl of the city.

Randomly, it is the staccato score settled.
But, under the guiding hands of digital homonculi
sweating out twenty-four hour days in silicon sweatshops,
it becomes something entirely other.

Here, the voices,
the petulant timbre of the quotidien,
the flatulent barking of the self-important,
the hog-nosed inquisitiveness of the aspiring.
Here, mired in the shit we sluice, is fertile ground –
the soil where managers reproduce.

It is not work: it is art.
We can sell it.

ii. Goodwill

*And as Slavoj Zizek argues, (according to Wikipedia) "the kind
of distance opened up by detournement is the condition of
possibility for ideology to operate: by attacking and distancing
oneself from the sign-systems of capital, the subject creates a
fantasy of transgression that 'covers up' his/her actual complicity
with capitalism as an overarching system."*
    *– Posted by Angela G. on October 4, 2008 11:29 AM,
        commenting on the 3,785 page Pirated Poetry Anthology
        at poetryfoundation.org*

War is a tubercular commerce carried out with other means.
Two dialects live in the country at war,
but do not define the front lines.
There is always mystery in both:
one is not a peasant-tongue or mud-clad demotic
clicking about the weather or failing bones and aches,
while the other hieratic touts
ineffable log-lines of foreign films.
No. They are both pierced through the heart
when war comes begging,
asking for alms for its campaigns,
asking words to salve its wounded.

They are the same heart, when the hammer drops,
smashing the tiny pot of seedlings saved for spring.
It ladles you naked into the garden of furies,
and so softly, for a hammer.
Take a picture & you are done.

The heart is the grammar of the annals of your body.
When your child's hand waves on conjunctions,
beckoning like a flic on the Place de la Concorde,
repeating "and and and and,"
whole languages leap like Renaults and Volvos
desperate to traffic in six revolving lanes.
These languages spill seed and flower and raw blonde roots
and nuts or shells shucked the day before or
nuts and shells shucked millennia after;
they fall from the back of the truck bound for market,
never to rest, restless,
invading the small borders of minds, mindful.
These languages, unborn, from your head
or two
or your child.
But you must give the child up to commerce,

trade him for the next child
whose dialect rings mute in your ears.

tympanum   type
trade   words

iii. Lessons of the Ninja Traders

There are no Steals or Lemons to squeeze.
Mere insectoid Scrabbling –
this whirring of wheels, wheeling of Deals –
is not good, not evil, not even beyond good and evil,
but is, rather, without Gravity at all.

You must find your Centre.
An American spell.

Hearken, you that would be Ninja,
hear in the night the terrible song of the shiruken,
and the mute footsteps of fate.
Know that the backdoor is always naked and vulnerable,
and that your greenest pasture is always someone else's
Backdoor.
Are you ready? Glean from your tools the passion
of death and the knowledge of life:
an Escape. A Dodge. A lucky break.
Always ready.

I understand now the role of my failed investments:
metaphors whose trade with the real did not pay off.

You cannot forge where memory has gone,
or pledge some feigned passion,
a muse who'll have no truck with you.

iv. Strategic Planning

A transcription of all the verbs from a speech given to open a conference plenary session.

FOCUS
looking grow challenge make celebrate work lag
    committed trust decided to
think created shared building
FOCUSSING
keep going responding look influenced impact
    deploying spend shame
capitalize capture spent reacting have recognize capture
    recognize
FOCUS
address position be
FOCUS
putting create collaborate listening
FOCUS
tell make sure
FOCUS
ignoring committed continue maximize indicated look
FOCUSSED
lookin' taking align want come aligned executing creating
FOCUSSED
think putting showing understand facing
FOCUSSING
understand try need
FOCUS
create
FOCUS
create talking like delivered billed waved created doing
FOCUS
follow measure become need gaining are gain holding
move viewed

reaching making taking connecting making mentioned
    to offer challenge
read post get receive starts align looking shared
FOCUS
guarantee meet begin taking
FOCUS
are
FOCUSSED
want
FOCUS
tell figure doing get need driving listen telling act think
are wonder anticipate anticipate share being have
contact facing anticipate sharing giving tell have need
need making making owe repeat account got work
embark mean challenge is is is is go back need exit
rising
FOCUSSED
look make asking
FOCUSSED
find make look forget increase work ask charge
shame get told move committed capture see do mean
    mentioned do make
make met know have understand have lead team see
    keep keep take take
FOCUS
be said connect network figure get take opt networking
    thank thank thank

v. Economy

If business class, crenellated,
seemed palatial, then your crown
lies buried in the sea, a submarine el Hambra,
bling of the Moors.

You cut the winds, hidden in the false virginity of the
    blue clouds,
the major chords of sun and sea recede,
haunting the tiny vale of this cabin.
This is part of what it takes.
They have seated you in a small aisle,
a precious handful of meal doled out to you.
Minister to your own needs.

vi. Reports

Comfort of instincts and confines of things.
They say they cannot redeem it, this cheque, this draft,
this is the nature of these notes black, these things
    broken.

From where it came, it came well, the nasty portolan,
the breakwater, grimped upon the seabed, grimped.
You know how it is, where the karaoke singers
ply their tawdry trade;
for them it is all academic,
for it was all something they could not rehearse.
I loved that aspect of it: that they couldn't rehearse –
there was nothing they could do but respond.
And when they did that, they could not reply
    haughtily,
but rather, like a naked peacock, they fell apart.

This is nothin' that they could feel ashamed of :
it just happened: they thought that this is what was
    required,
but we stayed softer on this point,
tried out a number of different processes and controls.

This qualified notion, this manic report,
this thing that tongued us into a lulled sleep, a place

where hierarachies thrived,
where named insolence only got you so far before
some frightened ape would send you back into the
    party.
... just don't revise any contracts with him,
don't approach the minister or any other members of the
    household.
Don't take this as a carte-blanche to start calling: I think
    we need to work out the logistics
because it is all so damn compelling when you are here,
you kind of think how there could be nothing else to be
    said for it.
You rejoice: the PowerPoints are valid, they are heraldic.
And you are green with the envy for which you
    are famous.

Perhaps this is simply too much for the meek;
more than we've budgeted for.
THIS IS SIMPLY TOO MUCH.
But it isn't enough.

vii. The Southern Love Song of Horatio Alger

Make for the undertakers
children from a tinsel cordon.
We seek the cab chits of a precocious fascist.

When I dance, I want you to remember
how the pieces fit together,
how the hunger of songbirds
can be tamed.

You are never alone in Virginia.
The ghosts descant the tune to a Gap ad,
Gibson's patterns spilled like blood
where our wars would have been.

Stonewall, crazed conflagration,
America will rise up in you for each generation,
take a picture of the past and tattoo it on your ass,
memento mori of salvation.

viii. Manufacturing Shipments Slide

"New data dim hopes of recovery."

The summer has closed.
The fall trains its winds
in small pools grown
in the upturned tables of sidewalk cafes
now fallow.

One very proper lunatic
plays with the turgid shit
left by the dogs
waiting at Starbucks.
He organizes offal
like a trader's stall
fresh from the kerb.

ix. Interest

They sold the whole boatload, coming into Charleston,
Lisbon the birthplace of the economy of the thing.
Mandelbrot's written the whole of it out,
can draw us pictures,
and so, fructified,
we can fall now, like hyenas,
heedless of whether the limb belongs to the prey or our
    neighbour.
The blood of the target,
hemorrhaging even the air, which sings darkly of our
    passion for knowledge,
how we want to understand the beast that nourishes us.

x. Mercury

You of the places
of the itineraries,
the Mercury of packets
of silver diaphanous plastic wrap
flash-frozen across the immanence of things.
You of the faceless visitations and
of being everywhere.
You of so many ways, angles and poems, and
your encyclopaedia of short-cuts and dead-ends.

xi. Penchant for Credulity (A Sucker Born)

Formica, in his telling, was more than surface,
more than pockmarked with cigarette burns.
That kitchen table, he confides, was the portolan of another,
    darker world,
almanac of the savagery that could be visited upon the
    working man –
that, and his penchant for credulity conjoined as
he missed the reasons. The explanations fluttered from an
    uncle's mouth,
flapped free of his father's lips
to gather and hang on the ceiling,
a colony of conspiracies in the growing twilight of the
    kitchen.
Bats with leathery wings wrapped to hide what they
    dreamed upside-down.
This was what he understood:
powerful men hated.

A grateful worship of outcomes,
like the accounting at Enron,
when minions in Finance shucked with pleasure,

awash in miracles of earnings:
yes, we are happy
with results.

xii. Secret Testimony

If only we did not name certain inconvenient rivers
(though we might navigate them nonetheless)
and instead abandoned ourselves to the bushy jungles
of truth.

We are prospectors, you see, prehensile people
who bend their bodies,
who graft such monstrosities
that we'll have the new races
we require for such atrocities.

In a ditch at the edge of her garden
lie waiting the cracked chromosomes
of a million alternatives.
Discarded now, perhaps;
but once they were a part of Machiavelli,
the Medici, another Nietzsche.

God laid low, a noisy DNA, along for the ride.
I never told her my real name,
wanted to keep her out of it.

xiii. Shining Path

She confides fantasies,
and they are not at all exciting.
Sometimes I figure as cannibal,
often as duped proletarian,
working long hours in the factory of her passions.
Maquiladoras of desire.
But I still struggle here, not conceding defeat.

Now we've taken to the jungles.
I cradle this Kalashnikov as my sex.
I believe
this is what she believes.

A trail of sap here, a pharmaceutical revolution,
covered with a thin pleat of soldiers.
Their helmets red in the mottled sunlight,
what little reaches us.
The jungle alone in us,
unlit,
actual.

xiv. Trademarks

The poem of commerce is fully-formed;
no hydra-headed beacon of chaos.
They send down squads of avenging angels
from Saatchi & Saatchi
and tear away the rough edges, the diacritical scratch
of the confused and mumbling,
stumbling in a twisted-heel cotillion,
leaving only the sincere oblivion
of your perfect genuine ass.

xv. Value

I will grow for you some ineffable rose, the mean
    of all roses: its lines
between all others, equidistant from every imperfection.

The average rose, then, where all roses would be,
were it not for broken thorns, torn petals,
the wind of their feet a sad, slow whistle.

When they run, these average roses,
they are like mountains, desperate for adventures.
When they fly, they contain the savage sky and read all
  the maps,
all at once! The average rose is something other.

The glory of it is in the colour: the mean of all sunsets,
the one that cannot occur for anyone yet.

Discharge Certificate

it was never about sacrifice   "the best damned
    vacation I ever had"

"being unable to meet the required military physical
    standards,"
you were thrown back into Canada at 25 years and
    five months
on the 6th of December, 1945
working backwards, you were five months pregnant

on your thin frame, dimpled with three years of war
my mother would have been an obvious conscript
clearly unable to meet the required military physical
    standards

you were issued the Canadian Volunteer Service
Medal and Clasp and the Defence Medal

the Discharge Certificate is signed
unbelievably
by Major Cock

Gun Reflex

We don't need gun control; we need bullet control. Each bullet
should cost five thousand dollars.
   – Chris Rock

A gunshot is no louder than a kiss.

The police are called,
but what do they know of guns?
The gun gelded, their disciplined, fettered guns.

Film is a virile gun:
it shoots a chick in a sword flick.
She knows the gun to kill Bill. Why?
We must kill Bill for love of other guns.

Gun is the black death of martial arts.
Armageddon for karateka.

A kiss is a gun with a mouth.
A car is a gun with wheels.
A gun is the career of passionate men who do not flinch.
A cat is a gun with fur, rubbing your leg to go out.
A bus is a place for guns to ride to their next killing,
warming themselves. Head against the sun through a
      window,
palms cuddled in their pocket.

A gun is the palace you could have had,
if only you'd worked harder, given more,
shot off your mouth less.

Guns are little things we say to each other
to keep ourselves in check.

Haiku Mo-Mo

The emanations
are not discrete; if a word offends,
pursue its issue.

PropertiesOf

We haveGrown a clearing
in our namespace –
what portion of things
we have felt we have
givenNamesTo:
'abundance', 'charity', 'dumb', 'greed', 'right', 'own', 'love'.

The work of the clearing itself
was monumental.
We had brought our Tools
but between the stuttered novels of morning light
and the stanzas of evening
we steeped them in forgetting.

And now they walk our halls,
mastersOfThePlace.

We still believe in cores,
hollowedOut brainScapes where a table
will sit still;
where the jagged edge can catch a sweater
or tear silk.

Essences smatter dark booty around
like the pirates they are,
nackered bastards sleeping on their swords,
and we gripe about them:
their singleFocus,
their utterReality.
We cannot be rid of them;
they split their genes with rusty daggers,
board the tidy merchant DNA heading for
grey and orderly ports.
They invest new biomes, raising flags.

ourHouse theirHome.
So we come now, after many years,
to the clearing again.
We have learned that on TV,
allReality evaporates,
and Essences waft towards theHeaven,
vaguerStill as they ascend the tempos,
where petty geniuses grapple them and write
logicalTreatises we cannot – nor shall ever – read.
TractataDentata.

So we have come to the clearing while everything
evaporates in hotSun.
We see imagosOfEveryThing rise, borne up
on their relative weightLessNess.

So that is that. And thenSome.

We reflect eachOther,
our namespace shriven, in earnest
each making for theOther
shapeMeanings and votive eye paintings and
allTheQuestions:
have you answered forEver
and have you?

We throw grappling hooks over the gunwales:
damn the torpedoes, we'd go in if it were even
        someSuch.
The cartouche prepared, signet rings and seals and
the heady deck of perfumed cards to take to the
        bottom;
to the bottom where the ropes connect,
the anchor has purchase.

It Thinks and It Suggests

how do you know, she whispers,
so soft,
between the funghi and calimari

oh, I know, he says
I know how he did it –
there is nothing special in that kind of success,
nothing you or I couldn't do, given a
general lack of squeamishness or
psychotic tendencies

he is interrupted. the lights come on
the police interrogate eyewitnesses,
they fear some conspiracy,
no one is talking. they leave

scales thick as dandruff on the afghan rugs,
tables strewn with comic-book skeletons of fish,
cats prowl the back alley, devoid of sentiment
feign feline disinterest in the world of men

it occurs to them now that there is a world
of vapours and breezes the cats and fish have been
    sharing
like a mystic tradition written behind them
underneath the chairs,
hanging in the red velvet curtains and the long sheer
    drapes,
everywhere there are blazons of war and hunger,
desire and death:
the haddock's eye now sends shudders through her
    spine

each vertebra a relay with electric plumage
she becomes a visceral addendum
to the shrinking diameter of bone that holds her head,
the waters recede and no longer do it for her
(cradle the cant of her head, that is)

he bites his lower lip, blackened
his canines grow thin, his incisors are needles now,
he bites his own tongue and it is sandpaper,
the room looms large
but he shuttles the warp and weft of it on four legs

a waiter brings the bill
and they pay with two cards,
vines of credit converging
a priceless euphoric sex

The Number of Spring

they are all good, unjaded people,
open to the language of self
to dread of irony
to tenuous green myths of transformation
to the number of spring

between leaves of grass
in truth, crawls instead the onomatopoiea of insects
beneath the emerald cowl lies breathing
the mechanics of birthing
and seed,
the mealy miracle of rot resequenced

and It happens, unbidden:
whorls grow in the roots,
write beneath the fulcrum of the stalk
which bears wind and the complication of rain
the health of merely expanding
the simplest, purest metaphysic

the examples of seasons past
unexplained anger or tepid loyalties
the Hun's hordes converging on Rome
the necromancy of fancy butchers festooned in black
    leather,
their dull minds drawing palpable lessons from the
    blue-grey acrid smoke

all the great tragedies
are so much run-off
when we count to the number of spring

Painters in the National Gallery

i. Ozias Leduc

What I find, in the mountain path,
is the leaf,
the leaves peripheral
to the path.
To see one from another
requires a child.
Come here, pick this up,
take this with you.
To the next leaf, a red-veined illusory ready-made in
    the snow;
you need to remove your gloves to get at its
    translucent skin,
to pry it away from the ice that was formed around it,
    and yet,
petty miracle,
did not encase it.
The next leaf is smaller, curled:
this one dried in the autumn sun,
worth deviating for,
leaving your parents talking on the trail.

Your hands are numb now, it is very cold
but there is one more, it is up over the hillock,
around the base of that maple that prods the wind with
    its bony fingers.
You make for it,
the snow is deeper here
and when you take it,
claim it from the branch,
you hear its stem snap with a crisp crack.

When you turn around,
the path is gone,
your parents' voices are gone.

Ozias Leduc, a road and artist,
knew this mountain well.

ii. Borduas

Having been lost for some time,
you look closely at the base of the trees.
You recall that you should be looking for the side of
     the tree
on which the moss grows.
But they are mere black masses, these trees,
mocking you.
They will not become your friends,
they will not become, in your later years,
lovers or angels,
they will remain
the frozen consolation of a random walk.

Bounty²

Nothing, this foam, virgin line,
to point out only the keel's cut.
So far off, upside-down,
a troop of sirens drown.

At Valvins, perhaps, mon capitaine,
your yole's³ pretty tongue laps little whitecaps
and the picturesque of your mind grows –
as a savage ice-white and blue crystal,
the beautiful of your thought grows
the azur Idea, the platonic Rack,
the Iron Maiden of Valvins.

To exist – that was, to stand out,
not as peacock's pulchritude,
but as the sail gives to wind:
balance, motion.

"I hear the songs, the womens' song,
the blithe songs of Paradise,
cut by Gauguin's hand."

"I hear a siren, mon capitaine,
singing of the bounty, the fruits that fall
faster than we can eat them.
Faster than we can know them,
apples drop in women's laps."

"I hear those sirens, Captain:
that, Captain Bligh – that is the thing –
I am in Hell – I am in Hell!"

"No vague white princess tarries there,
the sirens' counterpoint is skin,
dogs and pigs running, bleating,
the conch-shell roaring, your ptyx
a stye in no one's eye –
the drums are beating, Bligh."

We sail, oh my varied
friends, with me on the quarterdeck,
you the sumptuous bow that breaks
the tide of cursed things.

A fine rapture makes me,
undaunted by its vertigo,
bear upright this greeting –

Sanctuary, reef, star –
to Otaheite worth
the white care of our sail.

Poetry of the Turbo Era

Introduction

The son of Atreus was afraid and shouted out, "Antilochus, you are driving recklessly; rein in your horses; the road is too narrow here, it will be wider soon, and you can pass me then; if you foul my chariot you may bring both of us to a mischief."
— Homer, The Iliad, tr. Samuel Butler, Bk. XXIII

1977 saw the first turbocharged Renault chassis race at Silverstone. Its debut on July 14 of that year was inauspicious: unreliable, it became something of a joke and was dubbed the "Yellow Teapot." While its first few outings were unimpressive, Jean-Pierre Jabouille piloted the turbocharged RS10 to the first ever victory for the new breed in the 1979 French Grand Prix. This ushered in the Turbo Era: eventually, all of the period's front-running Formula One teams began recycling their exhausts using turbocharged engines. All hell broke loose.

Cars were not the only things that increased in velocity. Driver literary production hit an all-time high: where fans had acclimatized themselves to a trickle of haiku, the occasional epithalamion or the odd sonnet, the volume of work produced by drivers during the Turbo Era dwarfed the meagre – albeit highly regarded – canon established by the likes of Fangio, Ascari, and Clark.

But the question of why this was such a productive period has never been answered. Other works have attempted to chronicle the rise in literary fortunes of drivers in the eighties, but no serious academic forays

*have assayed the dense poetical thicket grown up in
the wake of the turbocharger. Perhaps there is little to
say: never had the leap between speed and death been
shorter.*

    *There has always been a literature of the Grand
Prix – inadequately recognized in critical circles,
perhaps, but there nonetheless. Take, for instance, the
following early prose poem attributed to the great
Alberto Ascari himself:*

An Exhibit of Photographs of Monte Carlo by Germaine Krull, circa 1936

The Germans did well that year, and, metal-death,
thereafter. The Mercedes and Auto Union rivalry had
erupted, Franco, into open warfare. Bugattis fell, chirp-
chirp, from iron talons; these delicate silver gelatin
prints capture the tenacious romance of race.

    The world of Monte Carlo was, that year, that killer
summer, that rapacious week-end wherein all the
death-forces of the continent had assembled
themselves, in a minor tumult. It was well-known that
the Germans were testing in secret, and that the French
manufacturers were finding it hard to compete. So
went the world.

    The Mercedes cowling was Futurism fanned into a
raging inferno: if you had no enthusiasm for this car's
bonnet, then you were soul-dead, deaf to the sensuous
pleasures of sheet metal smoothed as skin over the
carnal fury of the Merc's 640 bhp juggernaut. Evolved
from the necessity of carving air, these cars were
shimmering incandescence; the theological necessity, at

that time, of speed and all its promises. And its promiscuity: it had given, after all, to all the nations some hope, but had reserved its blessings for the Germans. All its doctrines and psalms became, in the blink of an eye, the hole in the air where the car had been, charging its way into the Tunnel.

Take everything at top speed because everywhere and anytime there could be a hole, a gap, an escape to get through.
   – Gilles Villeneuve's theory of racing, as explained to Prof. Watkins

Fear and Loathing in Montreal

While alcohol has certainly figured prominently in the lives of many a driver, there has never been a serious problem with psychotropics in the Grand Prix Championship. However, the following excerpt from Jim Bloos' **Amsterdam Diary** *suggests that a drug problem may explain what many thought was just a lapse in concentration.*

I cornered Frank Williams near the pit wall, and the drugs were beginning to kick in. His eyes were full of bats; the engineers sported bat headgear; the inane squabbling of FIA scrutineers was conducted in an inscrutable bat-tongue. All was possible now, I knew: grab these foul creatures by the throat, and then heaven, hell and the front row of the grid would just be the punctuation marks of a language even I, a rank amateur, could learn to speak.

But that is always the way with acid: your sense of what you are capable of not only outstrips reality (which is merely a problem of timing, as the careers of most dictators prove), it even outstrips the capacity of your imagination, so all you have remaining is the abstract notion of possibility itself masquerading as something you can achieve. In the middle phases of your trip, however, these ambiguities are filled in by very concrete hallucinations.

And you realize that narrative is not truth; it is power. It is about subjugation: forget the ends; we are talking means here.

If you think now about our metaphysics, the power of narrative becomes apparent. The history of metaphysics culminates in a massive simplification: the Void versus Chance. The biologist ontology is simple – and perhaps even true. It is not a question of Being; beings, simple variables in an algorithm of fitness, are agglomerations of Chance – aleatory patternings whose specificity may be unique, but are thereby no less provisional.

I must, you think, go faster.

Why had I been left here, to fend for myself, in a sea of red terror? I couldn't make myself approach the car. Christ, I couldn't even LOOK at the mechanics. I don't think it would be much of an exaggeration to say I broke down, which is pretty much how the press release ran: "More reliability problems plagued Bloos, with an unspecified engine failure the cause." Speculation was rife on Crescent St. that night: I had calmed down by then, but wasn't above torching some marketing knobs who'd been prescient enough to sport neoprene to the festivities. All just good fun and

games, gentlemen, I said, no harm done. And none
was. We are, after all, professionals.

Sequel to the Race

*Present, speed, sensations are elements which have always
seduced me. And yet I am unable to separate myself from the
slowness that is so necessary for writing and for reading, for
emotion and for desire.*
    – Alain Prost[4]

> *Jim Clark, the "Gentleman Driver," died in 1968. His
> work, however, prefigured many of the concerns of his
> literary inheritors. Clark's invention of the sestorolle
> form in 1967 in his piece "Sequel to the Race," broke
> the strict adherence to the tenets of Dada that had – at
> least in Clark's mind – shackled his predecessors to a
> spiritless and moribund absurdism.*

what Krull saw here
svelte shadows crease
the Casino characters
dancing like fauns
like children's eyes
peering through the armco

jade canticles sung
in the greensea tongues
remorseless sway
of the yachts' masts
yawing contralto to the
the raw-muscled roar
of 18,000 rpm

tyrannical sconce
hold my eyes with your fire
sequelle, sequine
physicist of the tyres
sestina, sestorolle
the circuit, inscribed in Hell,
in a path between doors
you in the grandstands
stand still as we come
riders on thunder
Sevillon, sarabunde
soliloquy
round the vaporous gate
without the tactile redemption
of all torque's tongue

Mechanics of the Death Drive

*While most literary depictions of the fan phenomenon
are laudatory – consider, for example, the copious
apostrophes to his devoted fan base in the work of Gilles
Villeneuve – there is nonetheless a bleaker strain that
first developed in the literature of the Ground Effects
Era. As fan affinities appeared to coalesce increasingly
around cars and teams rather than drivers, there were
some who began to glimpse the possibility that their
connection with their fan base perhaps had a more
sinister cast; that they were, in essence, parasites to the
relationship of adoration established between, for
instance, the House of Ferrari and its fanatical phalanx
of tifosi. The drivers taken on by Maranello's Old Man
all knew that idolatry of the red cars has often led to calls
for the head of any driver who failed their four-wheeled
steeds.*

*Patrick Tambay's installation piece **And If I Died For You?** was the first intimation that drivers of the Turbo Era were questioning the bona fides of fans' professed love. Clay Regazzoni, following his 1980 disabling accident and subsequent confinement to a wheelchair, had also queried the roots of this relationship in the serial tone poems he composed while in hospital. As he was to state in later interviews: "I heard in those first tentative experiments the slow drip of venom, and when I asked whose voice was responsible, I heard their cheers. I come back to you now from that experience clearly shaken."*

But it is the following piece, an "impossible" play written in 1982 by Jody Sheckter, that continues to haunt the very foundations of the driver-fan relationship, and serves as stark counsel to those young men who would sacrifice their lives to court the approbation of Grand Prix devotees.

SCENE 1

Inside. A dark room. A low-watt bulb hangs, naked, over a couch, unlit. A partially-clad man painted red lies on the couch. A TV plays upstage.

TV:	... Arnoux has passed Villeneuve, but there's no way that that's the end of it. Here comes the Ferrari again – they're wheel to wheel –
TIFOSO:	Where's the bloody telephone! (He scrambles to the floor and lifts a receiver from a pile of clothes.) Armando! Yeah, it's me. I know, I know. I want this on tape too. You got one? Good, make sure it's working, eh?

(A chorus of pit mechanics enters stage left.)

CHORUS: We are the dead. From where we stand,
            the salvage ketch of history has bled even
            Fangio's reknown dry. All this scavenged
            fame, the red cars dark demotic, the price
            of writing indelibly the word "Ferrari" on
            your tombstone, seems a trifle thin, a
            contrived spin into the pits; you are
            sheltering fear, harbouring the nostrum
            for your cowardice in these petty
            critiques of our handiwork.

TIFOSO: (Screaming into telephone.) Tell her to
            shut up! I don't care. Tomorrow, we go
            down there. Fuck Dario. Fuck, yeah!
            Right, tomorrow. Ciao.

CHORUS: When speed is sculpted in metal, who
                bears the will of gods?
            What Mercury now will outpace them?
            Are we to see fury drive the man?
            Or man drive Furies?
            Whose haunted diameter is the sheaf of
                cold steel
            that rams and pistons deep in the bore?
            What work where wheels wear road?
            What node nicks heart and kneels numb?
            What pass but pulling air past Lauda?
            What jump jerks foot to clutch
            to join the metals and the dead heat?

Message to the Mechanics on a Test Day

In the last corner I suddenly saw an image of Jesus.
    – Ayrton Senna, Japan, 1988

Ayrton has a small problem. He thinks he can't kill himself
because he believes in God and I think that's very dangerous for
the other drivers.
    – Alain Prost a year later, also at Suzuka

> *It is not generally appreciated that Ayrton Senna,*
> *arguably the greatest Formula One driver of his*
> *generation, wrote an astonishing amount of poetry for*
> *one who was so involved with the details of gear*
> *calibration and the near-paranoiac amount of testing*
> *that he commanded from his race team. His poetical*
> *oeuvre is notable, however, not for its prosodic*
> *achievements – although some would say it reads better*
> *in its native Portuguese – but rather for its*
> *inventiveness and its uncanny portent of his untimely*
> *demise. As one is tempted to say of Tupac Shakur, it is*
> *as though Senna had glimpsed the particular face of his*
> *own death and lovingly wrought its contours in the*
> *sinew of his verse. This early vision of mortality gives*
> *his work a weight and depth rarely seen in the poetry of*
> *Grand Prix drivers.*

this car, faster than lightning, is a killer,
a manic demon and I am
a priest at its exorcism, this track the path to God
behold, the everturning wheel
and the blip-blip-blip of the throttle
like a jejune parakeet
its throat the diameter of the popoff valve
the FIA is threatening next year
or a folksong customary to funerals

please
ensure the gear ratios are set up
I want to work on tyres only
tomorrow

Sestina: Altavite

> *Among the papers found after Senna's death is the*
> *much-maligned "Sestina: Altavite." Presumed to have*
> *been written in January of 1994, the same month in*
> *which he made his "I don't want to live partially"*
> *comments, the sestina added grist to the mill of theories*
> *that he had begun to lose his nerve.*
>
> *Proponents of Senna's religiosity liken its irreverent*
> *tone to the Book of Job; others, less inclined to preserve*
> *Senna's usefulness to the Church, insist that his lower-*
> *case god was a clear sign that he had, at least in private,*
> *distanced himself mentally from the notion that he was*
> *under divine protection. I would side with the school*
> *that makes of the "Sestina: Altavite" an apostrophe to a*
> *single, undivided deity: a monotheism born of being out*
> *front, alone.*

What I saw of Madonnas or Christs in that last crash
fits tidily on the head of a pin. As it should be with
    angels;
their humours, god-cant, mulch of perfection and
    spinning miracle wheel
were final distractions – the music of Tamburello's
    roar.
I would be where I was regardless; I lived only for the
    caress of speed,
only for the clear certainty of sitting pole.

It is a monomania born of no trinity, the pole:
it admits of no theology and is clear of the first lap's crash.
I would teach the children of the barrios this god-like
    speed:
outrun, outwit, out ahead, where you only tread with
    angels.
What you forget is worth forgetting in the crowd's roar:
always ahead, sharing nothing with those who grind wheel
    to wheel.

And if you should feel the bump and rub of your foe's wheel,
then, I would tell them, think of nothing but the pole.
Your blood become one with the engine's roar,
threaten him with knotted veins and love of the crash.
Make him fear the wrath of vengeful, angry angels;
make him lose speed.

I know some day some god may take away my speed
and my drive will shrivel like a heretic upon the wheel.
I will not go quietly; I will not stand by while that god's
    angels
prod my dying body with their icy, foul pole;
I will see my life done justice in the crash –
a goodly, terrible, final roar.

When as a child I tumbled from bedstuffs at a faerie lion's
    roar
and I dreamt all the dreams at dream-speed –
you know them, all the same – the silent scream and crash,
the fingers clamped like arab seriphs round the wheel,
and then Acheron's darkness. From where the dream
    runs down it, we pole
shallow-draughted to sit with bitter, second-place
    angels.

The Hell of not winning is what angels
will not let you see. So much for the roar
of the real. Focus on the pole,
focus on winning, on apex and speed.
Why let these critics and undermen wheel
out theories of where and when you will crash?

You hear the crash; the angels wheel
in their sky; you roar at speed to pole.

Scriptorium
for stephen p.

... we must ascend ourselves as emotive bridges.

We conspire with lightning to see.
Look, it is death, not poetry.
O blue shit of the Sphinx,
apoplectic artisan,
the desert could be your dead,
the sun the rising hour.
Here, those wizened jackals of Africa
or the dogs of your Morocco
would swell kennels
and we would toss them
poems of bone.
Gnaw the petrified spleen
of the last hunger.
Blessed mortal blossom,
all colours complete themselves.

I. Metamorphosis

The beginning, circular of movement;
we remain the rhythm, for the moment.

From the hushed flesh –
it is not for truth that I burn –
suspire, and the dark awaiting almond grows
in the seed of your lips.
We exchange the air for speech.

Through yawning azure, your breath ascends,
tendrils of text unwind;

I would lift my lines with the flame you suspend
taut and glistening, a canopy of fire.
A dumb huddle of woolstock,
my fleeced hunger gnaws,
my long and curling teeth descant
a white and clicking bonesong,
a psalm of flesh and blood.

By the brittle skin of this water I will write
for you,
by this lake, puckered as a navel,
by these rivers and opened mouths,
on this hill, on this rock.
The road will ring with traffic.
Our book, sweet Mother, our kingdom.

I will brook no quarrel with stone;
its instincts are sharper than choice.
First generations spent
as Pharaoh's tomb balances
this symmetry of sky and land.

Now the Tower came to be my body:
in the turbid swell
I float, eunuch, and the blood-foam
has no issue.

I dig around the keystone,
work designs that don't disturb
the growth in hanging gardens –
go deeper to the tomb,
touch nothing;
I would scratch for heaven
and send foundations deep.

You wonder how a world's weight
would sink it,

how butterflies would flutter
from under the wind.
We have dug these wounds,
chrysalids wound tight in white tents,
waiting for flight.
As I brush the sleeping dust,
there will be wings to rise
from these brittle homes.

I lay this page, sweet Julian,
altar for your sacrifice,
for the present demand of the past.
Cocoons cannot create,
but I bide time,
'til your warm tongue of life
comes licking at the worm.

I work the words and their spellings.
The words were here before you,
and will remain until ever.
Not that your hands build
history into the blind and bloody annals –
of this, we do not speak –
but that your body was your sword.

In every sense, the world is ready,
its silken glow soporific,
waiting for this labour,
a slumbering speech ready for you.

Mother, don't wail, Pharaoh's walls
came before even the cold steel spine
of sin pierced your tender, camouflaged wings.
And I was of the angelic choir,
my voice
a din
for butterflies only.

II. The Schreber Case[i]
exergue

*I make sackcloth also my garment; and I become a proverb to
them.*
    – Psalm 69:11

Do not sow doubt, leper,
do not bring stinking plague
to my house, to my people:

your hands, seeded with pustules,
sowing warts on the taut flesh
of this device I call
my faith.

---

[i]There is nothing even vaguely reassuring about the
case history of Daniel Paul Schreber. We can hardly be
placated by the various diagnoses of his illness; the
extreme rationalization he carried out concerning his
psychosis is perhaps only an anachronism – in
another era, he would have been designated a heretic.
There is a curious silence in modernity's estimation of
the "gifted psychotic" who provides for us his own
case history – the story of his slow emasculation at the
hands of God so that the "Order of the World" might
be restored – a kind of paranoid silence. Science finds
its ossified umbilical, stares at its own navel; it cannot
know itself. Freud's explanation of Schreber's illness
as repressed homosexuality manifesting itself as
paranoia is too convenient, and fails to take account of
many of the case's details. Freud himself believed
that, insofar as psychotic patients refused the analytic
transference so crucial to the "talking cure," the
psychoses themselves represented a very certain limit
for psychoanalysis. Kierkegaard knew this limit.

That is one response, one antiphon
for the blind and not naked.

The others are:
Who is this cannibal, this obscene maw?
Why this digestive concern?

Not until I am finished with them
am I finished with you,
so count the grooves
I hack in their fate.

It's grooves that catch the net;
if fish were smooth, then they'd be saved.
Thus fisher of men,
thus fisher of flies,
thus Isaac to be caught
in the stolid mesh.

To follow the way down,
the still leaves,
torn from the tree, believe in sunlight
while they rot, wholesome to the earth.

So drops the father's hand,
to the neck, naked to knife,
to take the son's life,
and the sun on Moriah stands
like the Ancient of Days
and spans one more minute
for Isaac, whose gaze
meets Abraham's, resolute.

So sons sundered from the root:
the modal visible interrupts,

so we misconstrue sacrifice for suicide
as the long teeth of agony begin their gnashing.

So daughters sundered from the root:
the long monologue of homicides –
Tiananmen, Kent State, San Salvador, etcetera.
Cain shit on the Order of Things.
Christ the spider,
limbs thin and stretched.
Fly, you hate his sticky web
and struggle to die.
Fisher of flies.

Der Fall Schreber – I am trapped:
what if the vision is not radiant?
Freud scratches with nail the board of bone,
Freud's dead fingers ravel scarlet threads –
my longing, his desire, Schreber's jewellery case,
Dora's reticule, all the boxes he wanted,
all the corners he could not have,
and the cold lick of a leathery tail:
he is the mother of our invention,
another prophet to stone.

Carry a lantern to the basic language.
Schreber mirrored, fondling his breasts;
he ties a ribbon, God appears.
In the basic language, God's gold lips let fall
the Saxon 'Luder', the English slut.

Carry a lantern to the opened book.
Beyond the bright tongue of talk's reach
there is a thing not baptised in light.

Christ the spider, fisher of flies,
His silver limbs glisten with dew.

Who needs these wings to hover
over the dung and dust of sweatshops?
I too will be glued to the crossing,
my buzzing silenced by strands.

"the human language (spoken aloud) ...
is the ultima ratio
for preserving the sanctity
of my house." [Schreber]

God crawled into old Abe's ear,
told him to knife his son.
God crawled into Schreber's ear,
whispered his longing.

i. The Basic Language

In archives, only the date reveals
the signature of the event.
A frothing maniac, the cold, dumb stare,
or a dream, once pallid angel,
now comes to paint the creatures
of a Lascaux of the mind.
The carbon dates reveal only
the manufacture of symptoms,
the date he went to press.

Our modernity pounced bleeding,
one with Schreber,
on the rent robe of passion.
The sign, perhaps, was Venus' crotch
propped open, a frayed bookmark beside it,
or the fat harangue of a kept art,
a bullet-hole sawn in plexiglass,
a Xeroxed report on the crisis,

the post-ings of bureaucrats,
the vital signs,
the vital signs,
the vital signs,
as if the dead need doctors.

ii. Homo grammaticus

He that would become
the Hyperborean woman,
the Jesuit Novice of Ossegg,
the Burgomaster of Klattau,
the Alsatian girl defending her honour,
the Mongolian Prince.

There is no subject in the clause of desire:
God's eye is a period,
watching, listening
to the sentence closing.
The damned automatic closing.
Those voluptuous claws closing.

The soft bird growing,
feather still wet
where the penis once was.
The little fawns playing,
their rumps golden brown.
And cats with gold eyes
sit silent in trees.
The Garden's asylum,
and the voices bring names.

How to write the end when, entwined,
the ribbons in his hair mirror

the twists and turns in fate's longing:
to become a woman,
the migration of sexes,
the dusty web on Mary's shrine –
Mother of God, to bring forth God.
Immaculate.

iii. The Case

The sacrifice:
steady, steady, bring hand to bread,
eat and see so steadily –

the blood of stellar bodies,
the blood of moon cycles,
spirit-rays drowning in your blood,
a crooked vine between your legs.
You open your sex to the lightning's tongue,
offer your eyes to the sun.

The date of the First Divine Judgement was the 2nd or
4th to the 19th of April, 1894. Things have never been
the same since.

*POSTSCRIPT BY THE SCRIBE WHO WROTE THIS
BOOK FOR JULIAN*

*Language depends on the most naïve of prejudices. Beware of
selecting only what you like, and leaving the rest. That is
what heretics do.*

III.

The Best Jobs

I dreamed I found you
not as you were
astounding and redoubled
in the glories of what you believe
but instead, a small dragonfly, red-tailed,
with wings dipped in a hovering grail

You came close to me,
whispering motley folk musics,
something, a reel perhaps, a line-dance
tuned to that hovering

I adjusted:
a rain fell equal
and the sum of your parts
eked a path through it

All angles and ascents
you poked your fever chart
'tween random and necessary leaves

Why did they outsource the easy jobs?

Organigramme

somnambulent prayer
the matter
conceptually divided
from itself
square stalls stacked and among them
hawkers of cures
and diseases

he recalls
the wisdom
of his infinite recesses

    building the homunculus
    from discarded
    conversational apparatus

he pounds the sullen vertebrae of sidewalks
noting exactly dimensions obtaining
in the pain of his body
    a fractured geography whose borders are
monstrous emanations from the spinal core

and he heard Sharp muse
his bald pate genetic:
    In the real world, one never finds an ideal fractal. One
    finds fractal situations – things that can be analyzed
    down to fractals.

where charcoal postponed its crystallization
for the dialectic
considering itself the very bone of Spirit.
natural repetition,
waves lapping the same seashore,
true internationalists

The arc described by the welder – clean fusing of
    metals – is repeated again in the sign of grace. It
    resides in the Russian doll's last house where she is
    eternally wandering, condemned to be repeated
    over and under in the infinite dwarfing of her
    interior spaces. When asked the question of her
    desire, she responded: "To have a God who grows
    smaller with me."

The government began to issue its own translations of
    Robbe-Grillet, whose sonority it recognized as a
    potential soporific. Eventually, Quebec adopts the
    Alain as its currency: "He represents everything,"
    said Parizeau, "even the anglos know that."

"At a certain level, I pass beyond hearing," she said. "I
    have no one to talk to."

eloi, eloi
what singing?
only halting locution, approximate samplings

his Russian doll tattoo
codes a theory of desire
a resolution
hardwired

here, he places phrases fusing
here, he fuses phrases placing
here, not so much here and now
only here
his insistence
        a manikin on a map

show me the Portuguese fishwife who does not desire
the interior spaces

the Franciscan friar who renounces
his cell

their voices recede to onion-skin whispers

notre dame de sous-terre and the words are tongues of
    flame on the very lips of the gargoyles, white noise
    on the amps of angels the hymns accelerated by the
    living stone itself through the hallowed hollow
    empty body of the Christus chez Chartres
    winnowed stone in the centre aisles guts of the
    organigram God moved in his entrails, the stone
    groans in its empty belly starved for light, hunger of
    the empty spaces

he remembers this now in the dim half-light
of Georgian Bay

represen.table
Plato threading form through
the eye of the Real

This is nothing, really.
variegated black clouds motionless in an hieratic font
a voice artlessly painted on the masks of trees
force manifesting sinewed articulations
bent where the bones are cramped and the vault of
    earth attends the waters
straight where fingers of wind stretch the sand to
    distraction
the Russian doll and the Black Queen, beneath the
    Janus gate,
mark with pins the voodoo map, influence of nations
but not here, these waters forgotten

in the night where all cows are black
he saw the absolute vacuum
opened and
advertised in the blank spaces
where there was nothing
but hunger

Hands are gone. Carved in delicate curves. considering
squat digits, mason's ideal slender indices, pointing
heavenward, grasping [bodies]. over history, hands
fall away. dust in the pews from the cold clutch of
saints
masons gone too far
in the shaping of angels
stone angles and recoils

les vitrailles d'aujourdhui

fractal
to inscribe the inside of desire
infinite maze in the middle of yearning
stretched, repeating
the lines of faces, repeating at their end,
in their valleys, sameness of
expression,
or each so in their result
the mouth of infinite tv
sameness in millions of households

sameness of the bees
sameness of the neurons firing, the ants
when congregating are said to have intelligence
sameness, altogether, gathers something to itself
begins to exert gravity
begins to mean in spite of the same
and begins

he stumbles upon an inner sanctum
6 meg of RAM, reflexes honed in Counter-Strike
homunculus, his desire,
in Medal of Honor, a repeated fractal compression of
    his likeness
inside world tv, the global village idiot
the first wave respawns
shifting continual virtuous perspective
zoom lens on the barrel, smudged at the edge
tidal extension of ganglia
lag, lag
in the Dis of a mind becoming,
damn lag
slouching in the bandwidths
towards him, repeated
headshot
himself [repeated]

The face, despite the too brusquely wrought contours
    of its details, nonetheless resembles you in almost
    every particular. The nose moves in a firm line from
    the single brow perched atop your eyes. They are
    set deeply, responsible in part for the dark enigma
    drawn in the registered latticework of pixels now
    responsible for your image.

*I have a feeling of man as part of nature and I'm part of nature
and I'm part of the life chain and I have to be sensitive to what
I'm doing and sometimes I'm not. Engineering has evolved to a
fantastic point. We have the flexibility to create some organic
forms. I'm talking about how forms evolve in nature, whether
it's here, in Ontario, or in the west. I don't think it really
matters. I would like to see our buildings very dynamic. They
should close up at night and then open to the sun. I don't see
why we can't have buildings that open and shut — that respond
to the sun and close to the rain.*
    — Douglas Cardinal

in the shade,
a shape again bristles
but indistinctly
and it may have been
struggling to inscribe in the night
the cold hieroglyph of its passing
but again, if this is vague,
it has at least been recorded
and the taut wires
singing
and the shadows extend their reach
and each phrase the two strollers speak is
in effect
a fractal
for when they return to the cottage, they will unravel
from suitcases, and unwind
the knots of conversation still lingering
from these – not pieces, not fragments –
but the real live bits
or the only ones that tend to repeat themselves
when the people are gone

Spheres/Real

i.
snow falls, cleaves
to trees
transfer of weight
from heaven

snow flakes, extrudes
cactus tentacles
remembers with slaked crystal tongue
its birth in water

the rabid world
waits, one moment
wonders
what is silent

ii.
fish stare
and for this,
they suffer
the displacements of water
snow the nightmare of all fish

iii.
snowmen,
right from birth,
consider all the angles,
wonder at the catastrophic warmth of possibilities

Deserts

i. San Diego

Petals folded in dusty seeds
blow, and blossom into San Diego.
Handles of Colts rasp cotton 'gainst my side.
I left the Presidio; walked to the Mission.
Air registers the choir's perfect pitch;
clear C# carries beyond carrion.
Uncloaked, the baleful eyes of dead horses
ignore El Cantico del Alba,
praise for the Virgin's intercessions.

Diegueños mete out the ration of the desert.
Sand their dance,
pellicules of earthcrust, their ringlet dance.
The night spastic,
a cold tourniquet for fevers and deliriums.
Dawn a refreshing religion.

Their star dance, any chance patterning
of tourmaline. Any Chinese star.
Priests my constant companions.
Priests, some holy, but others garnet-skinned,
tongues thickened with satiety of lusts,
limbs bent riding devils in this place.

In the town, they are revered as gods,
constant impecunity their apparent career.
But in Mexico, the Sheriff still seeks them:
cherubim of his post office wall.
His hot breath curling the posters, willing them
dead and buried, and their exploits void.

Bad priests: the will of Heaven, he thinks,
is their bad end.
We gather up our few belongings;
it appears I am serene and
duplicitous enough to join the fold,
to ride with 'em. Excellent cover, this cassock.

When we arrive in Tijuana,
an old woman works another warp in my fate,
there among the pigeons in the dusty square.
She hawks admonishments to pilgrims and
    desperadoes alike,
all advice a single refrain from the greasy leaves of her
    tarot:
"A fool and his money are soon good.
Bad money drives out all evil.
Money is the root of trees.
Money doesn't grow on everything."

The priests listen as she rummages under the custard
    paunch of her chest, explores and scours her armpits,
crepitus in her joints crisp like dried corn.
She implores them, reading their robes:
"Money isn't money.
Time is round.
Money makes the world go."

A lacquered sun wanders the desert sky,
cracks hard outlines from the incessant heat.
And the priests drink their fill at the font of this lucre,
contemplate a communion beyond imagining:
desire sieved and the desert filled.
They rub their hands together;
life-lines course their palms
like the San Diego.

In the sheriff's office, each bullet is arranged according
    to its perfection.
A lean and hungry man with a camera carouses with
    him.
He's bound for beyond the Rio Grande, to shoot
    Taylor,
which confuses the sheriff, as Taylor is becoming the
    hero of this Mexican war,
and no one is yet accustomed to this talk of shooting
    someone
who will live on forever.
The sheriff sides with the Mexicans, but doesn't let on.

ii. Las Vegas

Mallarmé marvelled in the textures of Vegas:
blackjack tables, pure altars.
He fingered the chips, their clay and serrations
cool to the touch, the graven currency of chance.
A makeshift Texan, he adored and enjambed
a speculation wherein
his eyes are death-heads
his dice are skulls,
and he throws in silence,
the brim of his Stetson low on his forehead,
his dark Ray-Bans reflecting the neon static of the
    casino,
slot machines stammering all possible metaphors:
a faded prayer
a bad cheque
a ribald ennui
a gracious winner
a broken cross
a sporadic deal
a random heartbeat

a quiet leaving
an anxious torment
a righteous tale
a manic experiment
a filthy vagrant
a taxing line
a florid emblem
of this sad brave hoarse-from-constant-championing
country of war.
Let us go down into death's stew mute and amiable,
let us call language's bet,
let us just receive our numbers in quiet and peace;
there are places waiting for us, and we don't require
this constant glamour of your chrome, or the savvy
　　of your indignation.
"Be quiet, I'm counting," he says.
And then he antes up.

Slow pan: the casino fix is in, he has its number.
He throws, his hand opens like a desert onion,
each skin in degrees echoes another neon exhortation,
and from its translucent lips speaks pollen across the
　　green felt;
the dice fall across tropes and anadiploses,
roll their improbabilities at the croupier –
the chuckwalla querying the Sphinx moth;
some silent banded snake secreting a volume of
　　antidotes
to the terror of abandonment in Death Valley.

The croupier shields his eyes and presses the small red
　　button
to call security.

He is tossed into the street because his failed prophecy
　　of language
has made him a hunted man; he's here now to take

what language would not repay.
The sheriff alive again, hunting him, his Colt Walker a
    form of cruelty.

[Captain Walker, namesake of the gun,
was killed by a lance at Juamantla, October 1847.]

A THROW

OF THE DICE

WILL NEVER ABOLISH

THE NEXT CHANCE

Out on the highway,
a red convertible carries, desperate in its trunk,
a heavy dose of the American Dream.

iii. Orlando

And then sat down on the leatherette seats,
set wheels to pavement,
forth in the gaudy RV.

So accustomed to the sound of death,
pay no heed when the next beetle
crashes into the glass, layers of brown jelly
and splintered exoskeleton spraying across the
    windshield
of the wizened Winnebago.
Death comes easily on I-87,
approaching Albany,
the plush teeth of America smiling:
the TripTik a conveyor belt of epiphanies,

an inexorable unveiling of essences.
Florida the telos,
where alligators roam backyards
and you must run zig-zag to survive.

Disneyworld is the dominion of our mind's eye:
occult ticket requirements debated like the Pelagian
    heresy.
My parents certain I cannot manage choice
without their guidance and example;
my soul certain that I am alone in this World,
and better for it. What I choose will determine
the value of the future.

It was not real, but it is real:
fuck Baudrillard, anyway (rest his soul):
he'd never been eight years old with a three-day pass.

Swamp-desert, whole tank-fulls of cypress trees
border my vision from the car;
there were killers on these roads once,
killers sprung orange, fresh-flecked with venom
from prison,
killers 'til the monotony of swamp claimed
their unslaked bloodlust and they fell in, chanting:
it's a small world;
after all, we are professionals, they said to the moon;
and the endless swamp blanket turned an edge,
furled them in, and their purple-ringed eyes,
that moments ago were dancing with panic
– from prison break, from the mania of a spree –
all these receded, and they entered the swamp
as the curtsying, wide-eyed children
of a sleeping mouse-god,
limbs tucked in as they turned their faces
to the watchful, sibilant moon.

So you approach Orlando on I-4,
shedding beetle skulls
and the unachieved furies of killers,
somnolent angels of murder.

Consider the swamp, which swallows with the vigour
    of sand.
Note the distances, the pilgrimages, the line-ups.
Walt wanted no one to think of the real world,
and circulated his oppositions at light-speed.
All the chances of light and dark,
of being and non-being,
of Mickey and Minnie,
war and peace,
history a small world, damn it,
after all.
A carousel of progress.

But my brother – six years old and yet immune to
certain fantasies,
certain desires that have not truncated him,
slashed and burned the ornithology of his desire,
so that he still knows the species and the predators –
he sniffs something foul.
He has begun to stress things.
When we turn corners,
he asks questions.

He asks us who is this cryogenized reject, "Who is
    Goofy?"
This terminal hick hypostatized,
this insipid model of everyman
refused by its maker, huddled in terror of its own
    breath,
terrorized by its own demonic dog-faced anthropic
    inadequacy?

A perfect sentinel for Walt – doomed to haunt the
    portals of magic,
the places where children's dreams come true,
but he can't even get a god-damned proper hat.

And my brother screams, sensing him around the
    corner of a building
and when my father looks, there is just scaffolding
and Daisy and Daffy sharing a cigarette
and there is nothing to help him; he shivers,
eyes rolling back in his head for fear of the buck teeth
whose glint is like the white death's-heads of the
    Pirates of the Caribbean.

For fear of the black upturned nose
that follows our scent, that finds us out no matter what
corner of Florida's swamp our camper drags us
    through.
I come to understand my brother's dreams,
in which Goofy with the body of an alligator
sluices through the swamp –
the perfect vending machine evolved for making
    dreams come brutally true,
sniffing for Vietcong and Alphagetty with equal poise
    and desire,
renegade sitcom and horrorshow,
grindcore demon and televangelist alike.
He knows no bounds, respects no visions.
My brother is right to lie awake at night, sweating in
    the campground,
fetid nightmare beside him, the full evolution of Goofy
come full circle as I find him in a pool of sweat,
delirium a-tremor in his eyes as he mouths the name he
    cannot speak.

I say it too, whisper so we can slide beneath the tent of
    dreams,
quiet to keep the killers asleep.

Infinite common dippy buck-teeth is
howling America,
draining swamps and finding bones of convicts
and birds, the crumpled walls of lost cities
and its bitter, bitter heart.

Fire in the Desert

at last the blazing sky
unsheathed Jeddah
clattered to the mirage's mirrored floor
like some tin angel
it lay before us, where we were berthed in the outer
    harbour
the heat of Arabia spawned its white houses and black
teeth of streets,
its unrelenting atmosphere, navigated, like the sea,
as a fathomless liquid by men whose eternal circumstance
seemed to be the aspect of a craggy shoreline,
indifferent to lack of wind or rain
navigated through merchants' booths with schools of flies
flitting between fronds of sackcloth and wood awnings.

Sherif Abdulla
tacks his mare, whose white mane hangs empty in the
still wind,
through these onyx streets without aspect. Shuttered.
Jeddah's silent respect, to him, is welcoming the
second son of Hussein,
Grand Sherif of Mecca.

that night
the tarnished brass of Abdulla's band honked Turkish airs
and held the heat
and "Deutschland uber Alles" rolled sluggishly off the skins
stretched in the damp air.
they warmed them over the fire and began again.
someone turned to Abdulla and said:
"It is a death march."
and Storrs spoke quickly
and laughter, flashing of teeth
returned
and the musicians begged to be sent home.

Almond

I am launched 4000 degrees:
all gained in plummeting through atmosphere
too colourful for paper words.
Red the certainty, the quiet virtue of tiny snails
tucked mute with foibles beneath the waterline.
Emblems of forbearance.
When the voyage began, self-same shells
crouched in tiny cabins,
cascaded conversations into nightdots.
Green unction of ocean swells.
Spread upon a beach,
calcium spectres of placement.
I say it:
an almond, in love.
The shape between all shapes,
but no letter is in an almond.
A field of hollows:
   abdgopq   and
a bridge of serrations,
serifed shelves to lay up piles;
but no almonds.
Let your hair feel green words
at the root of the almond tree.
Late love is coming; a place of four hands
and wild almonds; hectic love is coming like a
barked typhoon,
like a hot field of whispering.

Without Blue

Without blue,
Would the sky? Possessed of green
And yellow in their measures,
But without blue?

I speak across the ordinary table
To you in our argot of years.
It has red, green, blue in their measures,
And we take up the cup,
Drink long in each other,
Without green,
Without yellow and blue.

My Parents' Disxo

My parents' disxo spun when you touched it.

The cant of those boots,
black platform heels.
Three inches for my father,
finally taller than my mother.

What happened there, weekends gone?
I had seen her practice moves: my mother's disxo was
    nothing to be ashamed of:
the hustle, the bump.
Why were we shuffled to the aural gestalt
of my grandmother's Blue Hawaii?
Even Elvis was probably at my parents' disxo.

I knew some of the players, had met
deeply sideburned men introduced as uncles,
delivered highballs to their lithe wives poolside
while they careened through laughter
and winked at me as they took their drink.
Their polyester bikinis had no voice
in the Elvis of my grandmother.
I heard them over Donna Summer,
retreated to the plush bosom of a cream shag carpet,
put the albums on the turntable, turned the selector,
and rehearsed the moves.
I knew they'd love to love me, baby,
in my parents' disxo.

In my parents' disxo,
arguments over whether it sucked
seemed cruelly beside the point.

My father used his disxo to invoke the dead
and to reach deep with his new afro into the race
    consciousness
of all my Italian forebears whose souls shone in
glittering shards
in my parents' disxo as the ball turned
and he called to them in flared jeans,
invoked ancestral pride in his chest hair.
They had fun while disxo lasted.

The pool was a coffin.
Barry White, a dirge.
There were places I thought disxo would take people,
once they had given themselves to the music.

I remember one cold October afternoon,
coming home from school. Disxo was dead
in my mother's red-rimmed eyes.
No blue irony of eyeshadow,
no orange electric halter top.

Cary Grant's LSD Therapy
(after Lisa Robertson)

Conscious control can be classified as the marshalling
    of hallucinations.
Dreams become a battleground of old and new
    ignorance.
An anguish of ecstasy freed from shackles at the
    lessening.

The quiet of a room that releases the inhibition of an
    anus.
The force of mantras in their exquisite green finials.[5]
We are all over the floor.

I heaved Heaven and put in my papers for Hell.
Another time in one giant penis.
An ash grove merits the slow tundra of Romanticism.

Often crying is a philosophy.
I seemed to be a general menstrual activity taking
    place.
A philosopher once said, you cannot judge a sort until
    the night.

The necrotic miracles of this bureaucracy owe a debt to
    Fascism.
One hundred times the day became illegal.
Each session I used six hours.

My intention before LSD was to make myself happy.
Fascism lasted about –
He would be a fool to take something making him
    happy.

A man's many weeks of LSD, that didn't crumble to
    my delight.
My last youth, I was very dependent upon older men I
    found and women.
One day, I had a tough inner core of strength.

ENDNOTES

[1] Reds Bistro and Wine Bar (77 Adelaide St. W.) and Canoe (66 Wellington St. W.) are upscale Toronto eateries that would be perfect locations for corporate espionage. I assume that someone has already developed and is operating the Secrets Engine postulated in the poem. Small armies of operatives armed with clandestine recording devices (an iPhone would do the trick) would be deployed with explicit instructions to follow randomly-generated itineraries and record what they are able to overhear. These recordings would be uploaded every night and processed by the Secrets Engine to determine statistical correlations between the apparently random fragments of speech. This is why lawyers are cautioned never to use client names in elevators.

In the unlikely event that no one is currently operating the Secrets Engine, then please read Prospectus literally and pass it along to any venture capitalists of your acquaintance.

[2] "Bounty" is partially a translation of Mallarmé's "Salut."

[3] Mallarmé's yole is the sailing craft in this photo:

[4] Actually from Nicole Brossard, quoted in *Nicole Brossard: Essays on her Works*, ed. by Louise H. Forsyth, Toronto: Guernica, 2005, p. 33.

[5] "Architectural finials were once believed to act as a deterrent to witches on broomsticks attempting to land on one's roof. " – "Finial." *Wikipedia, The Free Encyclopedia*, 2010.

ACKNOWLEDGEMENTS

Thanks to

Domenico Capilongo, who ushered me into this; the
very good folks at Quattro Books; Allan Briesmaster for
his work, eye and ear; all the Really Good Poets
who've listened (Margot, Lynn, Joan, Shannon, Ralph,
Sonja, Liz, Norma, and Lois); Margaret Christakos for
making places and spaces to hear, read and think ...

This book is for Lise.

Poems in this collection have been previously
published in *filling station*, *The University College Review*,
and *COS*. "Scriptorium" appeared as Conspiracy of
Silence chapbook 002.1.

Other Quattro Poetry Books